WISDOM FROM YOUR ELDERS

Learning From Your Parents, Grandparents, and the Older People in Your Church

By: Patrick Baldwin

Copyright 2017
American Christian Defense Alliance, Inc.
Baltimore, Maryland
ACDAInc.Org

Special Request

Thank you for purchasing our book and supporting our Ministry. We actually have two requests – To Pray for Our Ministry and to Read this Book All the Way through. No Ministry can Survive without Prayers and Support so we ask you to keep our Ministry in Your Daily Prayers and Pray as the Lord leads.

We encourage you to Read the Book you purchased all the way through. Many Books NEVER Get Read, and the ones that do only get read the first few pages.

One of our Special Request is that if you are serious about learning the material in this book that you take time to actually read this book in its entirety – all the way through.

We all lead such busy lives nowadays and can get side tracked so easily, please take a moment to consider my words and read to the end of the book and keep us in Your Prayers.

Thank You once again for purchase. We deeply appreciate Your Prayers and Support and know that God will Bless You as You continue to Bless this Ministry.

Dedication

This Book is dedicated to those that have come before us and walked out their faith with fear and trembling before the Lord Jesus Christ. Your Wisdom, Inspiration, and Guidance along the way continues to bless us all. Thank you for serving the Lord and touching people's lives along the way. God Bless You.

Forward

Proverbs 1:8 says, *"My son, hear the instruction of thy father, and forsake not the law of thy mother...."* How many times have you said that to your kids? How many times did you *hear* that as a kid? Okay, so maybe not those exact words, but the message was the same: "Listen to me." "Do what I tell you." Or possibly even, "Are you pickin' up what I'm puttin' down?"

The words used isn't all that important. What *is* important, however, is that the message be both sent and received. Equally important is that the message be transmitted with consistency and regularity—by our attitudes, words, and actions.

This book is designed with the young person in mind. However, this book is also for parents, grandparents, and everyone else who has a regular connection with a child or teenager. Its purpose is to a) remind you that it is your job to instill wisdom and common sense into the hearts and minds of the generation coming after you b) give you practical ways to accomplish this task and c) help you do your job in such a way that it inspires and prepares the children and young people in your life to be ready to do the same...someday.

My prayer is that you will live the words in this book by applying them to your life in order to raise up a generation of young people who will be ready to:

- Lead the Church in sound doctrine and with the compassion of Jesus
- Establish Godly families
- Live lives based on solid faith and integrity

I know that sounds like a monumental-sized task. But it's not. All it really requires is for you to make a personal investment into the lives of the children and young people you know and love. So yes, while it *sounds* like a monumental-sized task, it's not. But it *does* have monumental-sized rewards.

Table of Contents

Chapter 1: Foundations of Relationships

We're going to start things off by simply looking at a number of verses in the Bible that address cross-generational relationships and 'discuss' how they apply to the world we live in today.

WARNING: some of the verses we are getting ready to look at are going to broach subjects like respect, honoring traditions, making changes, and embracing our roles. In other words, some of you are about to get a little uncomfortable. Or as my grandma would say, you're about to get your toes stepped on. But please don't let that keep you from doing your job the way God intends for you to. Besides, what's a little 'pain' when you know you will reap the rewards of your labor *and* be able to go to bed at night knowing you are making an impact for the kingdom of God?

So are you ready? Let's get started….

Children's children are the crown of old men; and the glory of children are their fathers. ~Proverbs 17:6

This verse paints a beautiful picture of the unity God intends us to have across the generations. It joins three generations together in a circle—one that is meant to be unbroken.

First let's look at the relationship between children and their grandparents (children's children). The Hebrew word for crown means to hold a place of honor or to be honorable. The responsibility here lies with the children's children (the youngest generation). They are to live honorable lives that reflect back on their grandparents in a positive way. In today's language, we would simply say, "They do us proud."

The last part of the verse places the burden of responsibility on the parents (the middle generation). They are to bring glory to their children—to be someone their children can count on...depend on...look up to.

Everyone has ownership in the relationship. Everyone invests. Everyone benefits.

One generation shall praise thy works to another, and shall declare thy mighty acts.
~Psalm 145:4

The message here is that each generation has a responsibility to bring their children and grandchildren up to know God. Not just know about him, but *know* Him.

Judges 2:10-11 is both a perfect and tragic example of what happens when we don't live according to this verse. Look at what happens...

After that whole generation had been gathered to their ancestors, another generation grew up who knew neither the Lord nor what He had done for Israel. Then the Israelites did evil in the eyes of the Lord and served the Baals.

People, the generation that was 'gathered' was the generation that crossed the Red Sea as children. They were the generation of people who ate the manna provided by God. They were the generation of people who grew up seeing God's amazing love as well as His anger displayed in some of the most amazing ways recorded in the Bible. So why, oh why, didn't they tell their children?

Why did they allow the next generation to grow up without knowing how and why they were able to live in the land "flowing with milk and honey"?

We'll never know the answer to that question. We do, however, know what happened because they failed to live out this verse. Israel lost its place of honor in God's heart and mind. They had their inheritance ripped from them and were handed over to the Godless.

Don't do this to your kids. Don't do this to your grandkids and to future generations. Set an example, teach with words and actions the value and essentiality of knowing God in a real and personal way.

Only take heed to thyself, and keep thy soul diligently, lest thou forget the things which thine eyes have seen, and lest they depart from thy heart all the days of thy life: but teach them thy sons, and thy sons' sons;
~Deuteronomy 4:9

This verse is another reminder—a warning even, against neglecting your spiritual wellbeing.

The first part of the verse speaks of the importance of being diligent in pursuing a relationship with God for *your* sake. You need to guard *your* heart and mind against apathy and sin so that *you* can experience the blessed life God created you to have. Moses was essentially saying, "Pay attention to what I am about to say and *obey...live by* the laws I am about to give you because they are from the LORD."

The second half of the verse is the multi-generational part. We are told to teach our sons and daughters these things. And just in case you've already forgotten 'these things'—'these things' being the laws and instructions from God given through Moses.

The laws and instructions from God referenced here are not limited to 'just' matters of faith and spirituality. It is a lot more than that. The 'these things' Moses was talking about was the entire Law (of Moses, as it is commonly called) that God set in place for the people to live by.

So while faith and matters of spirituality should be the foundation upon which everything else is taught, it isn't the only thing one generation is responsible for passing down to the next.

Hear, O Israel: The Lord our God is one Lord: And thou shalt love the Lord thy God with all thine heart, and with all thy soul, and with all thy might. And these words, which I command thee this day, shall be in thine heart: And thou shalt teach them diligently unto thy children, and shalt talk of them when thou sittest in thine house, and when thou walkest by the way, and when thou liest down, and when thou risest up. And thou shalt bind them for a sign upon thine hand, and they shall be as frontlets between thine eyes. And thou shalt write them upon the posts of thy house, and on thy gates. ~Deuteronomy 6:4-9

This is one of my favorite passages of scripture because it is so explicit and literal. There's no wiggle-room for misconstruing what God wants. No, what God *expects* of parents and grandparents. So let's take a few minutes to pick this verse apart and see what it is telling us to do.

Love the LORD thy God with all thine heart, and with all thy soul, and with all they might. Love the LORD with *everything* you've got. And do it twenty-four/seven.

…teach them diligently unto thy children…. The word diligent means to be thorough, persistent, conscientious, deliberate, consistent, and attentive. There's nothing happenstance or random about it. In order for this to happen, though, YOU have to be in sync with God. YOU have to be living what you speak.

The next few phrases in this passage instruct us to **talk about God's commands** when we are **sitting, walking, as we put our children to bed at night,** and **when we get up to start a new day.** Here again this is a strong and indisputable indication that God intends our teaching to come from *who we are* not *what we do.* It's lifestyle vs. compliance.

Example: Parents who pray with their children, pray for their children, worship and serve the LORD with their children in public, *and* who operate their marriage and home on the same principles are living obediently to God and to this passage of scripture. Parents who pray at mealtimes, go to church occasionally, or who are faithful attenders but the atmosphere of their home and their business dealings would indicate otherwise are not living up to God's expectations.

Putting these things on your hand and on the 'frontlets' between your eyes—now that's something you don't hear every day. These statements are referring to the common cultural practices of the day in regards to what the people wore. Translating it into something we can relate to, however, isn't difficult. Basically what God is saying here is that our appearance should reflect our relationship with God. We should teach our children to dress appropriately and to take care of their bodies.

We will discuss this subject more in depth later on, but for now, let's just say that while it isn't fair or even right to judge a book by its cover, our appearance does say something about us, so we need to teach our children to make sure they always send the right message—that they are a child of God.

Writing 'these things' on the posts and gates of our houses is simply God's way of telling us to make God's Word the foundation of our home. Fill your home with visible and tangible reminders of God's Word. But don't just throw a few magnets on the fridge, toss a pillow on the couch with a scripture verse on it, and buy a 'verse of the day' calendar every year. LIVE IT!

I have to tell you about an incident I witnessed in a store one day that is the perfect example of someone who surely had 'these things' written on the posts and gates of his home.

I was in a home décor store looking for something when I walked by a man talking to one of the store clerks. In his hand he had a wooden plaque with a scripture verse painted on it. I didn't think much of it, but because I was looking at some items directly across from them, I couldn't help but hear their conversation. It went like this…

Man: "I don't mean to be rude and I'm not saying this is your fault, but you really should sell this item like this." (hold the plaque out toward the clerk.

Clerk: "Why not?"

Man: "Well, because it's wrong."

The man then began to read: "In their hearts humans plan their course, but the Lord establishes their steps."

Clerk: "What's wrong with that? I think it's nice. It just reminds people who believe in God to have faith in him."

Man: "Oh, I know. And I'm all for that. I'm a preacher."

Confused clerk: "So then why are you telling me it's wrong?"

Man: "Look at the bottom. It says this verse is Psalm 19:16. It's not. There isn't even such a thing as Psalm 19:16 and the verse is Proverbs 16:9. "

Clerk: "Oh. Ummm…"

Man: "Like I said, I'm not trying to be rude and I know you had nothing to do with it. I'm just saying it's misleading. Or in my business," he laughed, "false advertising."

Like I said, this guy had 'these things' on his posts and his gates. And no, it wasn't just because he was a preacher. It was because he knows the Word of God.

This isn't to say grandparents and parents have to memorize the Bible or know it from cover to cover. But remember…you cannot live and you cannot teach what you do not know. So ready, study, live, and teach God's Word to your children.

That the aged men be sober, grave, temperate, sound in faith, in charity, in patience. Young men likewise exhort to be sober minded. ~Titus 2:2 and 6

These verses are part of Paul's letter to Titus on how to teach and train the Christians in Crete.

There are two things I really like about these verses. The first is that they clearly state the need and expectation for intentional mentorship by the older mean of the church to the younger men in the church. The fact that relationships are to be a part of this mentorship cannot be overlooked or dismissed. To exhort means to urge, encourage, and counsel (advise). These things cannot happen without being relational.

The second thing that sticks out to me is that these verses aren't limited to Biblical teaching. They don't let the older men off by telling them to make sure the younger men know how to pray in public, pass the communion trays correctly, and say a few 'amen's' at the right time. No, exhorting the young men to be charitable, patient, temperate, sober-minded, and faithful requires a lot more time and energy than could be given during a church service. Times haven't changed in this regard—not even since way back then.

Teaching the next generation of men to be charitable requires the old and the young to work together to know who is in need, what their needs are, and then actively participate in meeting those needs.

Patience—that's a tricky one, because patience is something a person has to do themselves. No one can give it to you or force it upon you. A person can, however, learn what patience looks like and its value on their relationships and life in general by seeing it in someone else. So by taking on challenges together (the old and the young) that require patience, and by simply sharing life stories and experiences in how exhibiting patience has served them well, the younger generation can learn from the older generation.

To be temperate and sober-minded doesn't sound like much fun, does it? It kind of reminds me of the old bachelor that lived at the end of our road.

He never waved or smiled when we drove by. The only person that ever came to see him was his sister. He was, quite honestly, an old grouch. But that's not what it means—not at all.

To be temperate and sober-minded means to be **calm, self-controlled, composed, peaceable, measured, sensible, and alert.**

Not a bad list of character traits, right? But let's be realistic. How many calm, composed, self-controlled, and sensible twenty-one year-old men do you know? I think every single guy out there over the age of forty would have to admit that their twenty-something self didn't always handle things the way they should have been handled.

But here's the thing—unless the twenty-something young man has a dad, grandpa, and/or other older men to look to, listen to, and learn from, he is never going to fully outgrow his impetuousness. He's never going to fully learn how to or the merits of:

- Thinking before he speaks
- Knowing when he needs to not speak at all
- Extending grace
- Knowing what actually is (and isn't) important
- Responding rather than reacting
- Empathy, sympathy, and compassion
- Being aware of his surroundings in order to keep himself and his family safe, to not be taken advantage of, and to know what is and isn't spiritually beneficial and uplifting
- Making sound judgements and decisions based on fact and Godly principles vs. emotions and peer pressure

In other words, young men need dads, grandpas, and other mentors to help them grow up in the LORD.

The aged women likewise, that they be in behaviour as becometh holiness, not false accusers, not given to much wine, teachers of good things; That they may teach the young women to be sober, to love their husbands, to love their children, to be discreet, chaste, keepers at home, good, obedient to their own husbands, that the word of God be not blasphemed. ~Titus 2:3-5

Paul didn't want anyone to be left out. So along with the verses we just looked at regarding the relationships in (and out of) the church between men of different generations, he addresses what the older women need to be teaching the younger women.

Women, too, are to be sober-minded. But when you are trying to juggle a baby, making sure your second-grader knows their spelling words, getting the house ready for company, taking your ten year-old to soccer practice, and trying to find time to get your Bible study lesson done…in case you actually get to go this week…. It's not easy to stay calm or respond instead of letting those knee-jerk reactions spew out. And showing mercy by dropping off a lunch box to the child who forgot their lunch for the third day this month—well, it's just not there. Not without the encouragement of someone who has been-there-done-that, anyway.

If younger women don't have older women to encourage them and remind them that this too, really will pass, they younger women tend to close ranks, talk (gripe) among themselves, and develop a don't-mess-with-me-or-I'll-make-your-life-miserable attitude.

Either that or one that gives up on seeing the joy and immeasurable value of her job and as a result, ends up bitter, resentful, anxious, and depressed.

Not a pretty picture is it? But it is a picture that never has to be seen if women will embrace the instructions of God's Word by taking the time to invest themselves into the lives of their younger peers.

Older Godly women can teach younger women to slow down and enjoy their children. They can teach them that a healthy *marriage* is something you never stop working at and that the kind of love that takes a marriage through a lifetime is something you *do*—not something you get or have.

These verses also place the responsibility on the older women to teach the younger women about things like modesty, purity, submission to their husbands, and being a homemaker. As I look at this list I realize most of these things are considered old-fashioned and non-issues in today's society. And if you are one of those people who feel this way, let me ask you this: How's that working for you? How's that working for society?

Excuses like:

- They (the younger girls/women) won't listen to me
- They (the older women) don't understand what it's like today
- Those rules are out of date
- That was for then—not for now
- I'm not a slave—I'm a wife

Anything along these lines simply don't let you off the hook. Hebrews 13:8 tells us that Jesus Christ is the same yesterday, today, and forever. He doesn't change. Neither do his expectations and commands—even if we think they should.

When Christian women from different generations join hearts and minds, life becomes better for everyone involved. God is glorified. The Church is strengthened and enriched. Homes are happier and healthier. Marriages thrive and last a lifetime. Children feel secure, confident, and know what it means to be loved unconditionally. In short, everyone wins.

When I call to remembrance the unfeigned faith that is in thee, which dwelt first in thy grandmother Lois, and thy mother Eunice; and I am persuaded that is in thee also. ~2 Timothy 1:5

This verse is yet another reminder to parents and grandparents that it is OUR responsibility to raise our children and grandchildren to know Jesus as their Savior in a personal way. It is a reminder to us that children truly do learn what they live.

So teach us to number our days, that we may apply our hearts unto wisdom. ~Psalm 90:12

And finally…in all of our teaching (and I am speaking here to the older generations), we cannot forget that we also need to keep growing and learning.

I was talking to a friend of mine about the fact that I was going to write this book. She then shared with me how blessed she had been in her years as a young wife and mother to be part of a small congregation that included a number of women old enough to be her mom and her grandma. In fact, she said, "One of them was my own grandma."

She went on to tell me how these women ministered to her and to one another. "I knew my entire family could count on being loved and cared for by these women. And not just at church. Phone calls throughout the week, birthday cards, hugs and kisses when we ran into each other in the store, fellowship in their homes…we had relationships. And the women who were what she called the middle generation—older than her, but younger than her grandma and some of the others—they looked up to the older women as much as I did. And they were ministered to in the same way I was."

Isn't that beautiful? That's what Paul was talking about in his letter to Titus. That's what God was telling the Israelites. That's what the Psalmist and Solomon were talking about. The Bible is filled with words of instruction on investing ourselves into the lives of those younger than us. So let's do it—let's be obedient to God's Word and raise up a generation of young people ready to carry on the work of the Church God's way.

Chapter 2: Benefits for Young People

What benefits are there for young people to develop deep relationships with their elders?

The benefits of spending time with your elders are both countless and priceless. Here are just a few (in no particular order of importance):

Respect

- The student cannot help but be humbled by the wisdom that comes from life-experiences and the teacher's appreciation and understanding of the need to be recognized as an adult rather than a child is renewed.

Work Ethic

- Older people are generally more industrious because they had to be and it was a habit they never let go of. Younger people need to understand that things haven't always been instant, pre-packaged, or ready-to-wear. They also need to know how to adjust in case they find themselves in a position of not having the luxury of everything at their fingertips.

Life-Skills

- I could go on and on about the negative effects of not cooking from scratch, making something from start to finish, and being self-sufficient when it comes to simple house maintenance, car work, and so on. But I won't.

Instead, I'll just say that when older men and women teach their younger peers how to do these things, the younger men and women experience a sense of accomplishment not able to be found anywhere else.

Tenacity

Giving up wasn't an option back then and the current generation needs to know it shouldn't be an option now. You don't quit a job just because you don't like it or someone hurts your feelings. You don't quit on your spouse just because you don't agree on how things should be done, you don't like your in-laws, or you don't feel validated and fulfilled. You don't quit trying to overcome bad spending habits, addictions, or a sinful lifestyles because it's too hard or it doesn't make you feel good. Older people know that there really is light at the end of those tunnels. So in spending time with them, younger people learn to keep looking for that light.

Wisdom

- Wisdom must generally come with age. Not always, mind you, but when God is in the equation, it is pretty much a sure thing. I know there are just some things we have to learn for ourselves—some mistakes we have to make for ourselves. But younger people can save themselves a lot of trouble, expense, and heartache by learning from those who have been-there-done-that.

Active Faith

- Faith in action can and should be seen in people of all ages. But when younger people are able to see active faith in older people, they are exposed to the aspect of longevity. Parents, grandparents, and older people in the church are living testimonies of the blessings that come from living a life of faith.

Once more, they can offer hope and encouragement in times of doubt. They can offer proof that the grief of losing a loved one does turn to sweet memories and hope for an eternal reunion. They can offer advice on how to hear and see God working in the lives of those that seek Him.

Unconditional Love

- By the time you get to the age where you are considered older or elderly, if you know God, you know His love is unconditional. Why else would you still be able to feel and experience that love, right? If it wasn't unconditional, you would have been gone a long time ago. Young people need to know this. They need to know that there is almost nothing God won't or can't forgive when we come to Him in true repentance.

This is something young people can't really learn from their peers, because their peers are experiencing the very same doubts. By reaching across the generations, older people provide tangible proof that no one is too much of a mess for Jesus.

Good Stewardship

- Older people know what it means to go without. They know full-well we don't need half of what we think we do. They know how to make a dollar stretch. They know how to improvise, re-purpose, and to live a more simplified and less stressful lifestyle. They don't have to have the newest and best and they know why you (younger people) don't have to have those things, either. In listening to their stories and watching their ways, younger people can learn to be less materialistic.

They can learn to recognize and appreciate what really matters in life. They come to learn that *"a parent's presence is far more important to a child than their presents"*.

Patience

- Again, this is just one of those things learned over time and experience. But when younger people hear someone older saying, "Be patient. It will all work out the way it's supposed to." Or, "Wait on God's timing and remember that God's timing is always perfect." it has a soothing and reassuring effect. It's like faith fertilizer.

Faith fertilizer—I like that, don't you? In fact, if I had to sum up the content of this chapter, this is what I would say:

Younger generations of Christians should take every opportunity to be friends with, fellowship with, serve with, and minister with (and to) their parents, grandparents, and the older people in their church. Why? Because in doing so, they get regular applications of faith (and life) fertilizer; causing them to grow and thrive spiritually and emotionally in the LORD and in their relationships with others.

Yes, that's it—that's what building relationships can do for young people.

Chapter 3: Benefits for Older People

Often times we think of these relationships as being one-sided in regards to their benefits. It's the younger people who learn new skills. It's the younger people who receive the attention. It's the younger people who are spared trouble and pain by learning from the mistakes of others.

The truth of the matter, however, is that parents, grandparents, and other adults have just as much to gain (and learn) from these relationships as the younger people do.

I think the number-one benefit is that the older person is fulfilling their role in scripture. They are being obedient to God. They are being teachers, disciple-makers, mentors, evangelists, parents, role models....Christians.

The next benefit I see is that of accountability. When I think of the accountability factor I think about the words of Hebrews 13:7: *Remember your leaders, who spoke the word of God to you. Consider the outcome of their way of life and imitate their faith. (NIV)*

You are being watched, mimicked and looked up to. And that, my friend, is powerful. Your words, actions, and attitudes are shaping those of the children and young adults in your sphere of influence. Knowing you have this kind of influence should keep you on your toes. No, you aren't perfect and you shouldn't claim to be. But knowing you are helping to shape and form the opinions and attitudes of others in regards to genuine Christianity should cause you to examine yourself more closely.

Parents, grandparents, and other adults who take the time to invest themselves into the lives of the young people they know and love, also set themselves up to receive the following

- Patience. Spending time with younger people 'forces' older generations to slow down to explain why. Explain why again…and possibly even again. Older adults are also reminded that their younger counterparts don't always know how to use tools or perform household tasks; requiring them to teach a young person how.

- Hope. This goes back to my number one benefit—fulfilling their role in scripture. Relationships between generations bring a sense of hope for the future of the Church to older people. When older people *know* they have done their best to teach, equip, and disciple the children and young people in sound doctrine and to be the hands, feet, eyes, and ears of Jesus, they don't have to worry about what is going to happen to the future generation. They know it is in good hands.

- Stimulation. Let's face it—parents, and especially grandparents, are sometimes guilty of being set in their ways. Fostering relationships with the younger generation keeps you on your toes. You stay 'in the know' (at least somewhat) on pop culture. You see things from a younger perspective. You feel younger (in an appropriate way). You consider and sometimes adopt a different mindset than what you previously had.

- Appreciation and respect for others. Listening to and caring about the thoughts and opinions of young people teaches you to respect them. You get an up-close and personal view of their intellect, compassion, and their desire to leave a positive imprint on society.

- Friendship. You can never have too many of those, can you?

- A stronger sense of purpose and usefulness. Relationships with people from different generations will allow you to share your knowledge, wisdom, skills, talents, and passions with others. You feel needed. Wanted. Useful.

Sharing life with people outside your generational peer group is a win-win situation for everyone involved. Don't you agree?

Chapter 4: Fostering Strong Relationships

Now that you have been reminded of why your relationships should reach across the generations, let's get down to the nuts and bolts of how to go about getting the job done.

What follows is a list of things you can do on the home front to form a stronger bond with the young people in your life. Just remember to be sincere. No one wants to feel like a charity case or an assignment. Be flexible and be yourself. Don't have unrealistic expectations. Give your children the freedom to be themselves too. Give the relationship to God and enjoy the blessings He sends because of it.

Tell stories. Sharing stories about your life when you were their age is a great way to connect. It also allows you to insert messages like "If I'd only known then what I know now" and "I sure wish I wouldn't have done that" all without sounding judgmental or 'preachy'.

Cook together. It doesn't have to be cooking. It can be any hobby or similar task as long as it allows you to accomplish something together. These types of activities are great for casual conversation and teachable moments. Don't let them get away from you.

Work together. Cleaning the garage, servicing the car, yard work-whatever needs to be done. Working together allows you to teach important life-skills and prepare them for when they are out on their own.

Teach a skill or hobby. Passing on the gift of a particular skill or hobby to the next generation has proven to be one of the best ways to solidify relationships with people of different generations. It's a passing of the torch kind of thing.

Volunteer. Did you know that schools would rather have grandparent-age volunteers than any other age group? There are numerous reasons why, but their wisdom, their sense of responsibility, and the students' positive response and interaction with them are at the top or the list. Teenagers like spending time with older grandparent-type people because they aren't always in a hurry to get to or from work or too busy to just sit and hang out and listen. Students also respond to this age group's storytelling method of advice giving better than they do their parents' more direct approach.

Chaperone events. You can build positive relationships with the teenagers in your life just by being present. When chaperoning events either at church, school, or in the community, you don't have to say much. Your presence sends the message that you are about them—that you want them to have a safe, fun, and wholesome environment to be a teenager. Your presence also says that you think they are worth your time and energy.

Cheer them on. Showing up for games, recitals, performances, meets, matches, etc. sends the message that you care. You are proud. You support them. You believe in them. Don't think they don't notice when you are there...and when you aren't. And don't think that just because they don't shower you with hugs and kisses they aren't glad to see you. They are.

Play together. Introduce them to the games and activities you played when you were their age and ask them to teach you how to play something they enjoy playing.

Pray for the children in your life. There is no greater gift you can give the teenagers in your life than to cover them with prayer.

Talk to the children in your life. Talking to your teenagers about current events, what's going on at school, what's going on with friends, and about what's going on in your life, as well. Don't confuse talking with inquisition. Talking is conversation *between* the two of you.

Listen to the children in your life. Listening is at least as important as talking. Listen to what they have to say. Ask them how they feel about things, what they think about things, and what their goals are. Listen not only to their words, but their moods and their feelings.

Give them ownership in their family's history. Telling stories about past generations, letting them know where their family came from, and making sure they understand the significance of family heirlooms is a great way to stay connected with the teens in your family. They need to know the personal and emotional ties to the pretty bowl they were never allowed to touch or to the necklace they know will "Someday be yours."

Ask their opinion and advice. Teenagers are really caught in a holding pattern. They aren't children, but they aren't adults, either. This often leaves them feeling disrespected and undervalued. You can solve this by asking their opinion and advice on things. They are far more tech-savvy than you'll ever be, so ask for their help. You'll both benefit.

Ask their opinions on current events and politics. If their mindset seems to be more world-focused than God-focused, you can then use the opportunity to discuss the matter in a calm, rational manner—and help them see things from a spiritual perspective. Ask them what they prefer to have for dinner one or two nights a week. Ask them if they would like to help plan (or be in charge of planning) the family's next outing or plans for their birthday. Ask them about…well, you get the point.

Include them in conversations and some decision-making processes. Yes, I know there are some things kids (even teenagers) don't need to weigh in on. But when it comes to things like where to vacation, whether or not to relocate, bringing Grandma to live with you, or how to tighten up the family's budget, allowing your teenager to weigh in isn't a bad idea.

Allowing them to express their thoughts and feelings gives them a sense of ownership in the family. It validates their sense of self-worth and the fact that you respect them. They do, however, need to understand that just because they are allowed to weigh in doesn't mean things will always go their way. This needs to be understood from the onset in order to avoid problems. But when handled properly, allowing them to be part of these processes helps build a more positive relationship between a teenager and his/her parents and grandparents.

See, that's not so hard, is it? Now get out there and start getting to know your teenagers better than you ever thought possible!

Chapter 5: Relationships in the Church

Below you will find a list of practical ways to build solid and lasting relationships between the teenagers and older people in the church.

Numerous youth in my life would tell you just how much of an impact these relationships have had on their lives. They would also tell you that there was nothing orchestrated or prefabricated about these relationships. They happened as a result of one or more of the following:

Teach. Who better to teach a group of teenagers than someone who has the knowledge and spiritual wisdom you have? Teaching sound doctrine and the message of the Gospel gives you the peace of mind that the young people of your church are being equipped to lead in the future.

Worship together. God intends the church to be a family. We can't really be a family, though, if we don't come together to worship God, the father of our family. Worshipping together creates a bond of unity with those around you no matter how old or young you are.

Volunteer. You cannot have relationships with people you don't know. Volunteer to chaperone youth group events. Volunteer to host them in your home for Bible study or for a special event. Volunteer to share your testimony with the teens during their weekly meeting. Volunteer to help plan and organize events for them.

Give. Donate your time and talents to provide food for their events. Remember—teenagers LOVE to eat. Donate funds so that teens that couldn't otherwise do so, can go to church camp, on a mission trip, or other such event.

Work together. Make sure your church includes the teenagers for church work days. Not only does it allow you to spend time together, but it gives the older people the chance to teach the younger people important skills.

Serve together. Don't exclude teenagers from service projects in the church. Serve together. Remember…the church is a family.

Pray for the teens in your church. This one needs no explanation. Just do it. And mention them by name. Additionally, when you take the time to get to know them, you will know what you need to be praying about.

Fellowship together. Again, don't exclude teenagers from times of fellowship with the adults by always having segregated events.

Use the teens in your church. Hire the teens in your church to mow your lawn, clean out your attic or basement, paint your fence, pet sit, etc... Having them in your home allows you to get to know one another and allows you to share Jesus in simple, yet meaningful ways.

Invest in their lives outside of church. Notice when their accomplishments are mentioned in the paper and compliment them for their achievements. Send them birthday cards. Talk to them at church. Ask them about school. Offer to tutor them or teach them a skill. Attend their extra-curricular activities.

Train them. Too often older people complain that the future of their local congregation is in jeopardy because of a lack of spiritual maturity in the hearts of the young people. Don't be one of those people. Instead, train up the teenagers in your church so that they will be thoroughly equipped for every good work (2 Timothy 3:16-17).

Give them responsibility. There's nothing a teenager hates more than being treated like a little kid. So don't. Give them appropriate responsibilities in the church. Let them be part of the praise team. Lead music. Offer public prayer. Serve communion. Work in the nursery. Teach or assist teaching younger children. Play on church-league sports teams. Greet people. Read the scripture publically. You get the picture.

Building relationships across the generations really isn't all that hard to do. Just like making friends among your same-age peers, all it takes is your heart, your time and a dose of effort.

Chapter 6: A Sense Of Responsibility

Among the things older people often fault the younger generations for is their lack of responsibility. They (older people) complain that their children and/or grandchildren don't have the same sense of responsibility they were raised with—that they don't know what it means to be held accountable for their actions.

I'm not going to argue against this point of view, because society and statistics prove that teenagers and young adults *are* less responsible than their parents and especially, their grandparents. But now I'm going to tell you something you won't want to hear: We (as in older adults) don't have anyone but ourselves to blame.

Over the past several decades parents have had the mindset that they needed to make things easier for their kids than they had it.

While that sounds nice in theory, in reality, it has created a generation or two of young people that neither know nor appreciate the sense of self-worth and accomplishment that comes with being responsible. That's right—we did it to them and to ourselves.

What to do? Fix it, that's what! Or at least, do our best to try—and here's how…

Set a good example by being responsible yourself.

Don't wait until your teenagers become teenagers to teach them how to be responsible. Okay, so that's the ideal situation, but if that ship has sailed, don't think it's too late. It might require more effort and patience on your part, but both you and your teens will be better for it.

Provide opportunities for your teens to practice and exhibit responsibility. This means that once you give them a task to do or mission to accomplish, don't rescue them.

Don't intervene and 'fix' things. Let them (require them) to complete the task or mission all on their own.

Allow them to experience both the rewards and the consequences of their actions. Responsibility isn't just about paying the consequences for the mistakes or poor choices you make. The positive aspects of responsibility are equally important— reaping the rewards of a job well done. Allowing teenagers to experience both is an important life lesson in decision making and for learning that they have the power to decide the direction their life takes.

Have realistic expectations for your teenager and expect them to live up to those expectations.

As I was typing that sentence I was thinking of Queen Esther. We don't know for sure how old Esther was when her cousin/father Mordecai, insisted that she step up and take responsibility for the safety of her people.

But history and cultural practices of the day tell us she was a virgin; indicating she was still very young—most likely in her very early teens—when she went to live in the palace and ultimately become the queen of the Persian Empire.

Mordecai's expectations didn't come out of nowhere or even out of desperation. He knew Esther was capable of carrying out the mission because he had raised her to be responsible. Yes, she needed a little encouragement and gentle prodding, but he knew she could do it **because he had taught her the hows and whys of responsibility.**

Can you say the same?

Chapter 7: Patience

I know, I know—patience isn't something you pray for, because the only way to get it is to have to use it. It's one of those 'practice makes perfect' kind of things. Patience is also something we all need in abundance; making it an essential character trait we need to help our teenagers develop.

Passing on the quality of patience is a lot like passing on any other character trait. It happens best when we show them how, give them opportunities to practice it, and expect them to exhibit it.

In teaching these things to your teenager, it is also important to make sure they understand what patience really is. The dictionary defines patience in the following way:

PATIENCE: the capacity to accept or tolerate delay, trouble, or suffering without getting angry or upset

Patience is also, and ultimately, learning to trust in God's timing and His will for our lives. Teaching your teen to be patient from this perspective is the perfect opportunity to help them grow their faith and grow in their knowledge of the scriptures.

David and Jesse are an excellent example of what this 'looks like'. David was just a boy when Samuel the High Priest came to Jesse; telling him God had chosen one of his sons to be the next king of Israel. There was one condition though—he wouldn't take the throne for quite some time. David would be king, but he would need to be patient and wait for God's timing.

David had no problem with that. In fact, in reading the last several chapters of the book of First Samuel, you will see that David even resisted getting Saul out of the picture on more than one occasion.

David's ability to wait patiently didn't just happen. It was the result of being brought up to know that God's timing and authority is perfect and worthy of our complete trust.

Some practical ways to help teach your teen to be more patient include:

- Model patience. I know I've already said that, but it's worth repeating.
- Work together on a project that requires patience. Landscaping, painting a room in your house, refinishing a piece of furniture, fishing, hunting, or playing board games like "Monopoly", "Candy Land" or "Scrabble", and gardening are all good patience-builders.
- Orchestrate delays that will require your teens to wait. Arrive early to an event. Serve dinner a bit later than usual. Tell them they have to wait until their birthday or Christmas to get their phone upgrade or something similar they want.

- Don't allow them to experience 'instant gratification' too often. Make them wait until they have earned the extra money they need to buy that certain pair of shoes or the jeans they 'have to have' because everyone else has a pair. Don't buy or serve fast-food or instant anything. Cook…from scratch.

In teaching your teens what patience *is,* you also need to be sure you teach them what patience is *not.* Patience is NOT:

- Allowing others to take advantage of you.
- Allowing people to habitually mistreat you, abuse the privileges of friendship, or disrespect you by ignoring your needs.
- Procrastination.
- Allowing others to consistently procrastinate at your expense.

How well are you doing in passing on the trait of patience?

Chapter 8: Faith

Previously I made mention of Hebrews 13:7 which says, "Remember your leaders, who spoke the word of God to you. Consider the outcome of their way of life and imitate their faith." (NIV) This verse is obviously speaking to the younger generations, i.e. young people in this instance, but at the heart of this verse is a message we 'leaders' must not miss. It is the message that leaders are to:

- Speak the Word of God to the younger generations
- Live a life of faith that is worthy of being imitated
- Serve as spiritual mentors to the younger generation by setting an example in how you worship, serve others, fellowship, and grow in your knowledge of the Word

Speaking the Word of God to the younger generations is essential for passing on and instilling in them the need and desire for a strong faith. After all, a person really can't put your faith in something you know little or nothing about. We can't expect the young people in our lives to live according to the Word if they don't know what that word is. What's more, we cannot and should not expect them to read, understand, and discern it all on their own. They need the wisdom and understanding that comes from studying over a period of time, aka age.

Jonah spoke God's message to the people of Nineveh. Peter spoke the message of the Gospel to countless people around him. Paul also took the Gospel to the known world of his day; preaching the message of salvation through Jesus. And of course Jesus himself spoke the message of truth to all He encountered.

Your way of life in 'church talk' is "your Christian walk". Are you setting a good example with your attitude? Your actions? Your speech? And I'm not just talking about at church. I'm talking about at home...at the bank...when you answer the phone and it's a telemarketer...when you are sitting in the stands watching them play ball...or any other public place. Remember: your *way of life* is just that—it's who you are rather than what you do.

Daniel's way of life caused pagan kings to know the one true God. Joseph's way of life allowed him to rise to a place of authority, which then allowed him to save countless lives. Barnabas' way of life earned him the reputation of being an encourager and dedicated leader in the early Church.

A faith worthy to be imitated...do you have that? I've had a few people comment over the years that they don't feel we should be imitating anyone's faith but that of Jesus Christ.

While I get what they are saying, scripture clearly indicates that we *are* to set an example and that we *are* supposed to be intertwined with one another in this way.

Elisha so admired Elijah's faith that he asked that it be passed on to him. Elijah, the faithful one, admired the faith of the Widow of Zarephath. Jesus recognized the faith of many; stating that it was their faith that allowed His miraculous powers to heal them.

So where does that leave you?

It leaves you with the task of being the Daniel...the Elijah...the Peter...the Joseph...the best You in the lives of the young people you are associated with. It leaves you with the responsibility to be a person of integrity and spiritual discernment and wisdom. It leaves you with the responsibility to teach, mentor, and live by faith.

Faith...it's what's best for a Great Life.

Chapter 9: Unconditional Love

Of all the things we should want to pass on to the younger people in our lives, unconditional love is the second only to that of desiring to know Christ as their Savior. The knowledge that they are loved unconditionally *as well as* teaching them the importance of importance of loving this way is the foundational cornerstone of living life as the hands, feet, eyes, ears, mouth, and heart of Jesus.

But what is unconditional love?

A friend of mine defines unconditional love as that just because you're you kind of love. It's the kind of love that doesn't depend on what you look like, what you do for a living, how athletic, intellectual, or talented you are.

Unconditional love doesn't notice how much you weigh, how much money is in your bank account, whether or not you have a speech impediment or acne, or anything else.

I've said it before and I'll say it again...passing on this and other Godly character traits is best done when you do them yourself...when you *are* these things, yourself.

Letting the young people in your life know they are loved unconditionally should really be a 'given' for any parent. Sadly, however, it doesn't always work that way. I think we all know someone whose relationship with their parents was performance-based. This simply should not be.

Jesus calls us to love as he loves (John 13:34) and Jesus loves us unconditionally. He didn't just die for the people who believed who he was/is. He didn't just die for the Israelite nation. He didn't just die for those he knew (because of His omnipotence) would someday accept him as Savior. No, Jesus died for *everyone* because He yet loved us even though we were sinners.

You need to understand, though, that unconditional love isn't a 'pass' that gives you the freedom to do whatever you want, whenever you want with total disregard for living a life of faithful obedience to Christ. Jesus loves us unconditionally but His blessings are conditional upon our obedience and faith.

For example, Jesus' love makes salvation available to anyone and everyone, but only those who accept that gift of salvation will be blessed with spending eternity in heaven. Likewise, the unconditional love that led Jesus to the cross is for everyone, but His blessings of comfort in times of grief, provision in times of want, and protection in times of danger are only given to those who are close enough to Him to receive them and recognize that they are from Him.

In the same way we need to let our young people know that there is nothing they can do to lose our love, but that if they want to be blessed in the relationship, they need to hold it in honor.

The blessings aren't a condition of our love, but rather a demonstration of our appreciation and joy for the relationship.

I hope this explanation is adequate. I also hope it is a solid reminder that loving unconditionally really isn't an option. It is a command from Jesus according to John 13:34. So as you think about sharing these truths with the young people in your life, remember to do it in such a way that you will reflect the Lord Jesus Christ in a real way.

Chapter 10: Wisdom

As you read these words, consider passing them on to the young people in your life in an effort to help them as they take this journey we call life.

NOTE: Some of the following words of wisdom are original, others are quotes (or variations of) many of you may be familiar with.

Don't ever forget or ignore your children, because they are your life's greatest accomplishment.

If it sounds too good to be true – it probably is.

If you have a Servant's Heart – You won't have a Selfish Heart.

Solitude brings Revelations

Everything is Possible but not Everything is Probable.

Think for Yourself and Learn Directly from God.

Pray for the Best but Prepare for the Worst.

Know Thyself then Be True to Yourself and Live with No Regrets unto God

Don't try to be anyone other than yourself because you aren't equipped to be anyone other than yourself.

Don't ever pass up the opportunity to be kind or bless someone

You get out of life only what you put into it.

When you have a bad day, just remember what a tiny speck that day really is in the big picture of eternity.

No one can make you do anything. Ultimately, you are the only one who can make you do anything.

If you spend your life thinking about what you don't have, you'll never appreciate and enjoy what you do have.

Speak the Truth – Regardless of the Consequences.

God's promises are never broken—we are.

God always has a plan and His plan is always best.

Say what you mean and mean what you say. Always – Let your yes be yes and your no, no.

Don't ever assume you know what someone is thinking or how they feel. Instead, ask them so you'll know for sure and then act accordingly.

Failure isn't a bad thing but accepting it is

God first—always. If you live that way you won't ever have to ask what's next.

God has promised us that in the end, everything will be okay, so if everything isn't okay, you'll know it's not the end.

Remember: Sharing life with the young people in your life isn't just a good idea. It's living life the way God intends.

Special Gift

God has a Gift for You!   The Plan of
Salvation:

There is no formal prayer of salvation as
many churches would have you believe,
God's Word is very clear - there is only one
way to get to the Father in heaven and that is
through Jesus Christ (John 14:6). Jesus says
that you must be born again to enter into
heaven (John 3:3-5).

Salvation is simply the first step in building
an open and honest relationship with God.
We all have sinned and fallen short, but
there is Hope in Jesus Christ - Just cry out to
God in sincerity and honesty asking for
forgiveness and for Him to Save you,
Sanctify you, and fill you with His Holy
Spirit - Ask for His will to be done in your
life on earth as it is in Heaven and That's it,
now just keep it real with God.

A Warning:

The Christian walk is not an easy life on the surface. The Word of God says that we will be hated in all the world for Christ namesake (Matt. 24:9). The Bible says that in the last days are enemy prevail against us physically until Christ returns to save us (Dan 7:21, 22). Furthermore, we must endure hardship as a good soldier of Jesus Christ (2 Tim 2:3) and yet we are never alone in this, God promises us that He will never leave us nor forsake us if we believe in him (Matt.28:20).

In everything we go through we have the peace and joy of God which surpasses all understanding (Philp. 4:6-8) The Bible declares, "For I consider the sufferings of this present time are not worthy to be compared with the glory which shall be revealed in us". (Rom 8:18). However, in all these things we are more than conquerors through Jesus Christ (Rom. 8:37)

Stay In Contact

Stay in Contact with the American Christian Defense Alliance, Inc. through Our Website At: ACDAInc.Org

Join Our Mailing List

We also Greatly Appreciate You Signing Up For Our Mailing List and Providing a Good Rating and review for this Book. Your reviews help other people like yourself find this book on Amazon and benefit from its contents.

If You or Your Family have been Blessed by this book please let us know by dropping us a line through our website at ACDAInc.Org

Find All Our Books

<u>Some of Our Books:</u>

Salvation for Your Unsaved Mom: 10 Things to Tell Your Mom Before She Dies

Embracing Pregnancy, Your Child, and Parenting: A Christian Parenting Guide to Offer Encouragement During the Wonders, Joy, and Hope of Your First Child

Parenting: How To Be A Great Parent And Raise Awesome Kids

Parenting Special Needs Children: A Christian Guide to Parenting Children with ADHD, Autism, Asperger's, and other Psychological, Behavioral, or Physiological Disorders

Kids and Prayer: Pray with Your Kids and Teach Them How to Pray

A Vague Notion: How To Overcome Limiting Beliefs of Fear and Anxiety Through the Word of God

Prayer: Your No. 1 Prayer Book To Learn
To Be A Strong Christian Prayer Warrior
That Prays With Powerful Prayers In The
War Room To Overcome And
Defeat The Enemy

Race Relations in America: A Christian
Guide to Unite Christians in the Faith

Martial Arts Ministry: How To Start A
Martial Arts Ministry

Biblical Bug Out: Don't Bug In - Follow
The Calling

Christian Prepping 101: How To Start
Prepping

How to Finance Your Full-Time RV Dream

Make Money: A Beginners Guide to Start
an Online Business, Work from Home,
Make Money, and Develop Financial
Freedom

Additional Platforms

Thank you for reading this book. Your support and the support of others continue to enable our Ministry to grow. We hope and pray that this book has blessed you. If you enjoyed this book consider purchasing it on additional platforms or giving it as a gift to someone who could benefit from it.

We have this book available as an E-Book, Paperback, and Audio Book. We have no way to know which platform you purchased our book on but want to make you aware of another way you can help support our Ministry if you haven't yet listen to the audio book version of this book.

If you Enjoy Listening to Audio Books in General Consider Signing Up For Audible.com. If You've Been On the Fence About Signing Up for Audible.com or Would Just like to Support Our Ministry By Purchasing Our Audio Book First – We Would Greatly Appreciate It.

Did You Know that You Can Support Our Ministry By Listening to Our Audio Books on Audible.com?

Here's How:

- Sign Up as a New Aubdible.com Member

- Purchase Our Audio Book First and

- Stay an Audible.com Member for at least 61 Days

If You Follow these Simple Steps Our Ministry will Earn $25.00 -$50.00 Every Time This Process in Completed. The Amount we earn is based on if we have narrated the book ourselves or outsourced it to another narrator.

We Greatly Appreciate Your Support as Well as You Sharing this information, including links to our books on Audible.com with Others on Your Social Media Platforms

Thank You Once Again for Your Support; We Know God Will Bless You as You Have Blessed This Ministry